THE WORM FARMER'S HANDBOOK

Begin Worm Farming: A
Beginner's Guide

Dr. Paul Ken

Table of Contents

CHAPTER 1

BASICS OF WORM FARMING

Vermicomposting, or trojan pony cultivating, is a characteristic, economical, and uncommonly compelling approach to make supplement thick fertilizer for planting. Worm fertilizing the soil exploits the normal arrangement of malevolent program assimilation. Cheerful, full, and crapping worms offer you with a point of fact interminable convey of great compost for your yard!

WHAT IS A TROJAN PONY RANCH?

Before you begin out PC infection cultivating, it is crucial to figure out how it functions. At its center, Trojan pony cultivating is a procedure intended to create supplement thick manure. This manure is useful for home gardens even as being far less muddled to pick up and less extravagant than other treating the soil strategies.

Customarily, plant specialists who need to apply manure need to either allow it gradually break down − which can be rank (and tedious!) − Or burn through cash on compost made somewhere else, which would quick be able to include (for the most part for people who like to do an assortment of cultivating).

WHY START RAISING WORMS

You are presumably astonished to examine the various endowments that hoisting worms can offer. Regardless of whether your issues are ecological, monetary, or green, PC infection cultivating can give broad expense to individuals who are willing to put in the exertion. In spite of the fact that there are numerous advantages that accompany bug cultivating, as indicated by our perusers, these are the 4 of the greatest huge:

1. Lessen Household Waste

Consistently, we produce gigantic amounts of waste in our homes. Everything from banana strips to old papers would normally mean heaps of waste discarded. Truth be told, it's far foreseen that Americans produce around 67 million tons of natural waste every year, and not exactly a third of that waste winds up treated the soil. Some portion of the purpose behind this is numerous Americans assume fertilizing the soil is excessively troublesome or not, at this point definitely justified even despite their time and exertion.

Regardless of whether you're intrigued by bringing down the natural effect of your family unit, or you like reusing what might some way or another be trash in a helpful manner, vermicomposting is by some separation one in all the best ways to deal with do as such.

What's more, not simply characteristic waste can be utilized. Indeed, even paper squander (comprehensive of papers and cardboard) assume a job inside the treating the soil framework.

2. Boundless Supply of "Dark Gold"

Any individual who has been cultivating for some time realizes that manure is one in everything about most monstrous expenses in local planting. By the by, the result (each as far as delight just as the monetary budgetary investment funds of developing your own foods grown from the ground) continually exceeds the expenses. In any case, consider the possibility that you can make all the manure you wanted for nothing. Wouldn't that make cultivating considerably more pleasant?

The fertilizer created from vermicomposting is classified "dark gold" for a reason! The discernibly supplement thick texture can flip even the most desolate soil (the sort of soil you'll consistently find in your lawn) into amazing cultivating soil. After some time, this "dark gold" can spare you stacks if not a huge number of bucks in compost cash! That spares time, money, and the environmental factors!

3. Important Teaching Opportunities

Vermicomposting is a super leisure activity to teach your kid too. It is straightforward enough that most extreme children can get it snappy, however also requires a degree of duty that demonstrates valuable not far off. Vermicomposting is ideal while it's miles kept up for certain minutes every day. It might be a remarkable other option (or expansion) to showing your child obligation through the consideration of a pet.

Not handiest that, anyway vermicomposting shows your little child the expense of protection. Raising worms acquaints them with the interesting and productive universe of cultivating in a manner they comprehend. Think roughly it: numerous children play inside the residue in any case, presently you can make it a beneficial undertaking!

4. Incredible Conversation Starter!

Worm ranches are well known in numerous pieces of the world. Notwithstanding, it's in any case an immensely new idea all through a decent arrangement of the United States. In the event that planting is something that you appreciate talking roughly with your companions, vermicomposting might be a fascinating and productive expansion in your discussion.

CHAPTER 2

ADVANTAGES OF WORM CASTINGS

Worm castings create the incredible manure inside the worldwide. Not handiest are they made through a totally natural procedure, however they likewise give the perfect equalization of nitrogen, phosphates, potash, and the entirety of the other plant nutrients that your yard wishes to flourish. Obviously, presently not all worms are the equivalent, and the Red Wiggler PC infection is through far the fine PC infection for vermicomposting.

The PC infection housings themselves are the final product of the stomach related technique the worms go through. The material itself positively blends into the dirt of the trojan pony ranch, delivering the particularly esteemed manure.

In case you're stressed which you're by snare or by law breaker disturbing the regular procedure through gathering the malevolent program castings, don't be! Worms don't obviously flourish fine in their own castings, so you'll unmistakably be helping them out each time you collect new compost for your yard!

Some various favorable circumstances of bug castings include:

a. Completely non-harmful and naturally delivered compost elective

b. Less scent than various composts

c. Studies recommend that manure made with worm housings can have as much as multiple times additional nitrogen, 7 cases the potash, and 1.5 cases the calcium of ordinary soil.

IS WORM FARMING STRENOUS?

In a word: NO! Worm cultivating is positively exceptionally smooth to inspect. That is the reason we urge you to prepare your adolescents how to do it; it's an excellent ability that is extremely possible by method of even hugely small children. So as to make a trojan pony ranch, you should simply follow some simple advances:

1. Construct or find a compartment – The initial step is to discover a field (generally wood

or plastic) to keep up the ranch itself. While it's far attainable to fabricate a field yourself, financially delivered holders are progressively dependable after some time, and make certain to not meddle with the characteristic strategies of the trojan pony ranch.

2. Fill the holder with appropriate sheet material – Before including the worms, you'll need to fix the compartment with wet paper (or another reasonable sheet material), at that point transfer a couple of basic soil, both that you purchased or a not many that you

have just got in your outside. The field itself should be sufficiently wet to keep the dirt inexactly stuffed, yet not all that wet that the worms are powerless against suffocating. It is additionally gainful to add egg shells to the dirt (when you have them).

3. Populate the homestead with Red Wigglers – This part is genuinely basic: truly transfer the worms for your field. Try not to stress an extreme measure of over putting too much (or insufficient) into the homestead, in light of the

fact that the worms will self-adjust their people truly rapid.

4. Give the compostable texture – Compostable texture can be the entire thing from food waste to the remainders of garden cutting. The basic standard right here is: in the event that it deteriorates normally, it might cross inside the homestead. Nonetheless, there are some particular assortments of fertilizer that should never again be set into your PC infection ranch. These suppers include: dairy, meats, citrus, fiery fixings,

fats, oils, and vigorously handled nourishments.

5. Keep up and reap the homestead – While it is basic no longer to overload your worms, keep up in musings that your worms need to devour a ton. Truth be told, Red Wigglers eat about portion of their weight every 24 hours, which implies you could transfer new suppers in your worms every day (this is an uncommon activity for adolescents!). Make sure to cut the dinners into the littlest pieces you can. Likewise, avoid setting dairy

and meat into the homestead. These are harder for the worms to process and may make a remarkably more regrettable smell.

CHAPTER 3

WHAT DO I HAVE TO START WORM FARMING?

Vermicomposting is uncommon in light of the fact that it doesn't require a lot of a speculation, and gives tremendous profits rapidly.

Worm fertilizing the soil receptacle

While you may actually utilize basically any case as a bug fertilizing the soil receptacle, some will be some separation higher than others. Industrially made compartments make it some separation less hard to hold new layers of your homestead, and could be far more noteworthy dependable than something you make yourself. We have some malevolent program containers accessible in our on-line shop that are improved for the natural concerns stressed with vindictive program cultivating.

As we referenced, not all worms are best for vermicomposting. Red Wigglers are by far the fine alternative because of the reality they produce the right mix of supplements for planting. While it's far impossible that you may find Red Wigglers in your terrace all alone, they are exceedingly lower valued and to be had on our site. For the expense of a sack of manure, you could have the animals you have to make your own compost in interminability.

To the extent required parts, you'll have the option to manage with only a container, worms, and the crude materials your worms will devour. In any case, there are various additional items that make worm cultivating less troublesome, and help development your yield (usefully obtaining themselves after some time). Having the rigging you need to guarantee your ranch has the best possible temperature, dampness, and pH forestalls errors and spares you money not far off.

WHY FARM WORMS?

Manure is a significant asset in any nursery. Indeed, even in a little space, compartment cultivating could be less entangled while you could make as a base a portion of your own creating medium. In huge nurseries, manure is a need. It let you verify that your dirt stays refreshing and fit for giving significant returns. Luckily, you could make fertilizer even inside the littlest of spaces.

A malevolent program ranch is an awesome method to make fertilizer and bug ranches come in all sizes. Worms can assist you with breaking down kitchen squander into a striking soil-improving material, loaded with supplements with an end goal to help your vegetation to develop.

CHAPTER 4

SOURCES AND RESOURCES REQUIRED FOR WORM FARMING

Luckily, beginning out with PC infection cultivating, or vermiculture*, is less entangled and economical than you would conceivably envision. The monetary cost will be little and for best a little interest in time; you may get a raised yield from your nursery and will shop a portion of your kitchen squander from going to landfill. On the off chance that you expend and cook supper with clean foods grown from the ground this will be a lot of waste, on the off chance that you stay purchase your dinners equipped made, it's going to absolutely be less.

All you have to get started is a field for your worms to live in, cardboard and vegetable pieces out of your kitchen. When you set up a bug ranch effectively, the worms will to a great extent adapt to themselves. On the off chance that you give your worms the correct environmental factors you could leave them to their own special devices for consistently or two while you proceed onward trip and will handiest have invest a touch energy in suffered upkeep.

PURCHASING YOUR WORM FARM

The principal component to consider is the holder with the goal to save your worms and fertilizing the soil materials. There are a lot of less expensive PC infection ranches available, however to shop money you may likewise think about building up your own. Worm ranch pressing holders come in numerous selective sizes. How gigantic your container must be will rely on how bounty supper's squander you make each week. (Overall) you'll need cycle 1 rectangular foot of PC infection container surface. How profound the container must be will to a great extent depend on how tons bug throwing fertilizer you need to make. A few people select a crate with different plate or vertically isolated compartments, while the best forms have doubtlessly one major region for the worms. The materials utilized normally depend upon what a man or lady needs to hand.

A few gatherings move the keeping up of bug homesteads and make them to be had at a decreased worth or perhaps for nothing out of pocket. (City of Sydney Council and Byron Bay Council in Australia both give PC infection ranches at a forceful rate).

You can likewise are searching for out an advisor who helps with the hardware, setting up and redesign of the trojan pony ranch. Here in Byron Bay we are blessed to have Compost Central, mounted by utilizing Andrew Hayim De Vries who gives these contributions and ability.

BASIC FEATURES FOR YOUR WORM FARM

A worm ranch need to permit your worms to breathe thus, clearly, can't be hermetically sealed. It must be a cool space on the off chance that you need to not warmth up an over the top measure of but then so as to offer worms with a definite measure of security contrary to the virus. The worms despise light thus the holder should reject as parcels gentle as attainable. While not really basic, many worm ranches have an isolated supply at the base to incorporate overabundance dampness and keep the worms from suffocating and a tap to purge off that fluid. (The fluid would then be able to be utilized as an in vogue thought process plant feed.)

CHAPTER 5

WHERE TO SITE YOUR WORM FARM

A Trojan pony ranch might be kept inside or outside, despite the fact that the key's to pick a space wherein the temperature will no longer fluctuate too uncontrollably. Worms will perform wonderful at temperatures among 10 and 25 levels Celsius despite the fact that the most generally utilized species can keep on existing somewhere in the range of 0 and 35 degrees.

Precisely in which you region your PC infection ranch will depend upon the territory you have available to you and the climatic conditions wherein you remain. Whenever spared accurately, your Trojan pony homestead might be an independent unit and will no longer make monstrous scents. It is a smart thought to save it close to, despite the fact that now not in, your kitchen. This will make it less troublesome and quicker to take care of the ranch with supper's scraps.

SETTING UP A BED FOR YOUR WORMS

Before getting your worms you should make a bedding for them inside the holder you are the utilization of for the pernicious program ranch. Layers of destroyed cardboard or destroyed paper could be perfect thus. Worms will rest between the layers of cardboard or paper. At the point when wakeful, they may then test into by means of into the food scrap layers, eating their fill and discharging the bug castings that will shape the reason of the fertilizer that you'll make. This bedding should be wet to make the correct degrees of dampness so as to permit your worms to live to tell the story. Including a little amount of manure will help worms to adjust to their new residential.

WHAT KIND OF WORMS TO USE IN YOUR WORM FARM

The worms in your PC infection ranch are not a similar kind of worms that you'll situate inside the dirt of your nursery. The master treating the soil worms most normally utilized are Eisenia fetida, Eisenia andrei or Eisenia hortensis. In more sultry atmospheres, there are some extraordinary bug species which can be higher prepared to deal with the tropical temperatures. Vermiculture specialists might be fit for propose you on the top of the line species to use in which you live. Worms inside the correct circumstances will raise snappy. For the normal family unit, beginning with 1 pound (simply under ½ kg) of worms will for the most part grant the populace to repeat and quick satisfy need, however obviously you can generally start littler and develop your way up. A solitary individual or couple may best require around 1/2 this amount.

SOURCING WORMS FOR YOUR WORM FARM

fertilizer worms

In Australia, you can undoubtedly discover and arrange worms in your PC infection container on line. In positive territories you may likewise be equipped for find neighborhood providers. There are some of companies who will distribute worms to wherever in Australia.

TAKING CARE OF YOUR WORMS

Worms will devour kitchen vegetable pieces similar with their own body weight every day! On the off chance that you have half of kg of worms, at that point, you'll have the option to manage half kg of waste each day. Obviously the amount of kitchen squander that you could take care of in your worms will increment in light of the fact that the number of inhabitants in your bug ranch develops. While including food in your worms it's miles good to start languid after which step by step development the sum. In any case, transfer just ½ a pound of scraps each subsequent day. Continue looking internal your canister consistently from the start. In the event that it begins offevolved to smell – you have overloaded the worms. Essentially quit including suppers till the smell disappears. Taking care of pretty much nothing and often is higher than including tremendous segments of dinners squander in one go. While including food, ceaselessly ensure you transfer it underneath some cardboard or paper bedding. Worms will rest at the zenith of the heap and dive underneath to eat up. Covering the food waste will furthermore lessen the probability of organic product fly issues. Here is a posting of one zero one issues to take care of your worms.

DAMPNESS MANAGEMENT IN YOUR WORM FARM

Worms need a high water substance to remain. They inhale through their skin and may do so most extreme effectively while their pores and skin is sodden. They will flourish while the dampness stage around them is at around 75%. When keeping up worms for treating the soil it's miles pivotal to forestall the vindictive program ranch from transforming into waterlogged or drying out. It is for the most part a decent idea to hose down the bedding, except if the pieces you have conveyed have a totally unnecessary dampness content. A case with a store at the base and a tap to exhaust off additional fluid will make it less confused to ensure the dampness content material of the field isn't excessively unnecessary.

THE END

www.ingramcontent.com/pod-product-compliance
Lightning Source LLC
Chambersburg PA
CBHW051405150726